Marry

&

Burn

Marry
&
Burn

Rachel Rose

HARBOUR
PUBLISHING

Harbour Publishing Co. Ltd.
P.O. Box 219, Madeira Park, BC, V0N 2H0
www.harbourpublishing.com

Cover illustration by Jorden and David Doody
Edited by Alayna Munce
Cover design by Anna Comfort O'Keeffe
Text design by Mary White
Printed and bound in Canada

Harbour Publishing acknowledges the support of the Canada Council for the Arts, which last year invested $157 million to bring the arts to Canadians throughout the country. We also gratefully acknowledge financial support from the Government of Canada through the Canada Book Fund and from the Province of British Columbia through the BC Arts Council and the Book Publishing Tax Credit.

Cataloguing data available from Library and Archives Canada
ISBN 978-1-55017-718-3 (paper)
ISBN 978-1-55017-719-0 (ebook)

For Isabelle

Contents

III. Addictions

I.

Vows

Anthropology

Family was the unit of measure for our people. We practiced CrossFit;
we hung from ropes and jumped from boxes. We brought squash
into the house and carved monsters into their rinds. We walked many
miles; we suffered; we bound our feet in hide. Marriage was a four-
day feast and an exchange of goods between households. The bride
was captured in her bedroom and dragged by her golden hair to the
merriment of all. When a woman gave birth, two women held her
legs at the knees. A rope was tied around her husband's testicles for
her to pull with the pangs. Even if she died, she died silently, not like
women now. If the infant couldn't grip a pole on the third day, we
left it by the river. We gave the mother herbs to quiet her. When a
woman reached the age of sixty, we cut the skin around her face and
stitched it on, tighter. We made death-masks out of wax. The ball was
round and made of leather. Beer was consumed in great quantity. The
winning team got its pick of females of the land. Our eyes were the
colour of milk when we could no longer see, black tea when we still
had sight. Brush was cleared by fire. Children were held down and
ritually scarred. Without this mark they would be unrecognizable
to us. Elders were venerated, except in times of famine, when they
were left by the side of the road. We wore uncured pelts. We urinated
in the rising dust. We urinated on the festering wounds. We spread
honey on the goiter. Women could bare their breasts but not their
buttocks. If a woman showed her hair or skin, certain men were
allowed to beat her. We performed sky burial. Our women glossed
their toenails with red lacquer. We put flowers on the graves of the
dead. We collected the blood of animals in glass bottles. We made our
own marriage ceremony in which a man could become the beloved of
another man. We made powerful magic in the caves above the sand
dunes. We made sausage. We ate the silver fish caught in baskets. We
washed in the sacred river. Our hieroglyphs were folded in papyrus.
The boys memorized the stars and the girls the forest paths. In the
mornings we copied sutras. We read a paper of bad news. Some
directions were taboo. Black was the colour of death. We possessed a

machine for blowing leaves from one side of the street to the other. The sun was a laughing goddess who split her vulva for the other gods to admire. White was the colour of death. We wore the greased wool of sheep and boiled their sour milk. There was a pyre on which widows were expected to leap. Our roof was corrugated tin, thunder when it rained. The women's priests injected botulism into their foreheads. A man had as many wives as he could carry. Mothers with their hair in ponytails drove children to soccer games. We kept a bear in a cage until it was time to bring him to knife. Sometimes we married the slaves we caught in war, sometimes we cut out their hearts on the stone steps of temples; it depended on the way the bones fell. Lattes were carried in the left hand, car keys in the right. If twins came, we took them to a certain place in the forest and walked away backwards. When we couldn't have our own, we went by airplane to receive a baby for which we paid generously. We roasted whole goats, under heated rocks. We never touched that which was *tref* nor a bleeding woman. We left everything in our wills to a refuge for orphan dogs. The smoothest stones were placed in the mouth of our wombs. We trimmed the edges of our lawns with silver scissors. Feast days were very important among our people and the women were proud of their curries. A certain cactus gave us courage. We made fortunes on trading in fractions of seconds across time zones. We appreciated sunset walks by the water holding hands. Without vodka our government would collapse. We shipped bull semen across time zones. We vacationed in hot countries, worked in cold ones. The only universal was bees. Bees and love. Honey and sting.

The End of I

Go through your manuscript and take out all the "I"s
—Not I's editor

I is passé. I is post confessional. I is gender
fixed. In the boy's section of Addictions-R-Us
I begin to panic. I is transfixed. I cry with mine little I
something that is crystal.

Aye-aye, captain
                my captain, unfortunately for I
                        I hoist I
on I's own petard.

Bide a while, love, sigh
softly in I's arms. Tell I the truth. No, hush.
You and eye are star-crossed.
I walk softly. I carry a big
book. I is conditional. I clap
one hand in the forest

I fall I blink I is a cat
in a poisoned box.
I is dead I is also alive I is paradox.

I speak in tongues, I art chaos theory
and you art my beloved departing
by several hundred horsepower.

Eye is unflinching I is
break-hearting, I pray.
I swing low, Aye
burn lye, I turn to thee
in the night and there
between you and I

13

breathes the secret that will do us divisible.

What kind of *Verschränkung*
is this? I put a spin on it,
we are so polarized, I and I's love,
immeasurable distances between us,

dare I say galaxies

the entanglement of our sheets,
the state of our marriage,
where both dead and alive are possible,
where a raised eyebrow changes the weather.

I your godspeed, lightspeed,
theory of relativity.
Make up thy fucking mind: Take me back
or leave me.

The End of Love

Into the quivering dark I walk
to the track. Grass purrs, whiskers of frost
squeak under foot. At home you dream
your solitary secret, the end
of love. I feel but do not yet
know. Loop track, chuff of breath,
chapped cheeks and ears, cold-forced tears
at dawn's birth crowning, the first folds
of blood shed into the groaning arms of cedars.
Slow double beat of wings, grey
over black, slapped air startled to life.
A hawk with a gripped and wounded crow
flying upside down below.

On the frost-furred lawn
the hawk lands, hunched like a quarterback,
wings sheltering the black flap's weak ragtime.
Another crow flies low, surveys:
a single scream and it's a flash mob scene
a murder at a murder. The sky's cauldron
tips a black storm to swarm the harried
hawk, call, *Shame! Shame!* Dawn has come
in flame. The hawk holds on with one talon,
screws the other deep to the heart
like a man pulling on a tight black boot.
Crows graze its crown
hurl curses, but the hawk hunkers down
tears clean to meat. Kill blow.
I am in a crow snow globe
the world off-kilters, tilts to spilt milk.
Three strikes I'm out.
I spread my arms for simple balance.

Blood and feathers, sudden
clarity. Daybreak. The cold
walk back.

Marry or Burn

Here is the gown undone. Here is the cost of the stone.
What the priests would say to men: marry or burn.

Turn her in your hands, lick him like a stone.
Where the ocean roughs up the sand: marry or burn.

Turn to her in pain, touch his body of stone.
Faces roughed up by years: marry or burn.

Rune your midnight fears, rue her stone loneliness,
she who cannot be blessed: marry or burn.

Yearn for sea surge, cliff-crash—any storm
to end this slackening calm: marry or burn.

Urn your stillborn ambition, worn like water on stone.
You made your grave, now sleep in it: marry or burn.

Who are the men, the women you might have become?
Who might you have known and loved? Marry or burn.

Turn it in your hands, knock it against stone:
the key is lost, you can't get in: marry or burn.

Once she dreamed your name. Love is a zen koan.
You're the clown with a greased smile: she's the nun. Marry or burn.

It hurts like a tidal wave coming home. It hurts like an unset bone.
Mourn, mourn! Marry and burn.

The Flight

Welcome aboard Humanity Flight 101. Fasten your seatbelts.
We have sealed the doors. In preparation for takeoff
we have betrothed you to your neighbour.
We have made you foster father to the baby
sobbing in the seat next to yours. Fasten your seatbelts.
You must purchase your own bibles, your own beverages,
your own toilet paper, your own prayer beads.
There will be a fuel surcharge for the obese
and atheists. There will be a fuel surcharge for babies
and those who made them. Fasten your seatbelts.
Your height-weight-proportional stewardess will
soon start the beverage service
prior to the weddings, which will begin in first class
and continue to the last row before the restrooms.
Do not throw food. If you are already married,
be advised that FDA regulations have annulled all prior
contracts. You are entering thin atmosphere. Pressure may change
without notice. You may be searched and detained, but not
expelled from the craft. Fasten your seatbelts.
If you and your betrothed do not speak the same language,
fill out form FCKD-10 in the seat pocket in front of you.
Language lessons are available on board on channel 2.
If you think you have inadvertently been labeled "Lesbian" or
"Vegan," you may ring for assistance, but if we run out of
entrées or fiancées we cannot guarantee your first choice.
We wish to advise you that putting on your own mask first
and then helping others is a myth. All passengers
must hold hands and hum Kumbaya during turbulence.
Our captain is fully armed
and licensed to perform weddings
divorces, circumcisions and dental extractions.
The Milky Way is a myth. Extra-terrestrial life is a myth.
We are alone with each other. Fasten your seatbelts.

All air is recycled. God is a myth.
Turn to the person
on your right and say,
Nice to meet you. I am your betrothed.
Expect turbulence.

Flood

Once Sappho wrote:
Do I still yearn for my virginity?
Once I would have answered no.
Later, yes. Now I simply yearn.
Delicate: once your fingers touched petals
to my paleolithic hips.
Remember the way we loved, before
what we now know came? Pangs of spring,
season of remorse and runoff.

Fractured, at a great distance,
because she was lost in translation,
they allowed Sappho her monstrousness,
her deviant grace—
even as they try to beat us normal
in the common era.

Sappho, I said no until you stopped asking,
and a dike in me broke, flooded the chopped fields.
Instead of yes I fed you honey, crushed the comb
against your tongue, wax in our mouths.
Sweet my heart, the four chambers of poetry.
Fire. Flood. Monsters. Maidenheads.
Cuts lifted from stone by tongues of rain.
Whose kingdom for a membrane?

Come, you said, flinting me with your Sardinian gaze,
let's make a myth. Once I passed beneath
your brazen linens' pomegranate stain

on my way to the fountain. I knew just what
his hands knew, unlocking the door to the well.
Spring, bitter as an uncured olive in my mouth—
I could scarcely carry my measure of water past your threshold.
O then, O since, O vernal equinox.

Why let husbands come between us
when your hair, bright as saffron, fills my hands?
You were so stone
I flooded.

Honey

The artist covered his nude
subjects in honey, then photographed them. It was
wasteful and terrible and unforgettable.
Such varnished vanity,
torpor of living amber cloaking
the naked body, slow deliquescence
preserved. This is how I loved you.
Honey. Didn't I, fully and sweetly,
pour myself over you? Didn't you
bow your head under that thick and holy
light, that slow weight? No sting,
only the glistening beauty of the moment
captured, and after,
unseen, the sticky, private struggle
to come clean.

Cleave

Perhaps it was a mistake to buy you the ring
the week you asked for a separation. August swelled
with heat, loops of onion fell from my knife.
The children knew nothing of such sorrow.
My face streaked with sudden rain
I served them lies:
No, loves, it's the onions—she'll be home late.
We touched each other
like curators in a museum of bone shards.
I separated our clothes. As I burned
in the guest room beside my stacks of poetry,
the ring kept its golden eye
open in the socket of its hinged box. It winked at me,
kept me from sleep.

Our country forbade us from vows,
then gave us permission to marry
but not divorce. I couldn't catch up
to history.

What would we have worn to the ceremony?
Everything that happened was brutally private.
I paid for the loop of gold
that let me dream of a different ending,
a ring that owed me wishes,
which will be one wish spoken twice:
Don't cleave.
A ring that turns into a keyhole,
that opens the door back to enchantment,
but your fingers refused the tradition.
Cleave: I cling. You unstring.
You sever. You halve. You rend.
I clasp. I cherish. I ring—

Once two girls castled themselves in a tower
and wrote their own story
but you were also the joker
who became the squire
who became the knave
while I was the milkmaid
who became the lady of bridges
the princess of crows,
embroidering hausfrau: how
did our legend fail?

I return the fool's
gold untried: we are gathered today
to divide, dearly beloved, to witness
your great loneliness unmarry
my veiled pride.

The Affair

Who knows how it began?
We know exactly how it began.

Who could have stopped the hand of fate?
We stopped the hand of fate.

When did life become so full of pain?
Life has always been a bed of pain.

So help me God, where were we going?
We were going to the shipwreck and the storm.

Why did we succumb to each other?
It was slow as a train wreck and empty as an emergency.

How long could things go on like this?
Like this: a man and a woman. An end

and a beginning. A car in moonlight
parked in shadows. He wiped the tears

from his glasses, tipped my face to the streetlight.
One of us said *body,* the other answered *family.*

One of us said *touch me,* the other whispered *poetry.*
We were old enough to perjure.

I leaned in to the leather of his coat.
Gently we looked at each other, we pressed

the places that hurt together.
Say it, poet, what you do: *I burn.*

And believe it, poet, what you live for: *to burn*.
No, my lover with indifferent eyes didn't ask when I'd be home.

The Addiction

We were a thing. We lived in the corner of Montreal
where trash blew in, where grit bit the heat of bare skin.
Everyone was bilingual
but spoke French first, because politics.
You taught me French of the body
I was the amuse-bouche, yes, *j'étais*
bouleversée.

There was someone else for each of us.
I didn't find her lipstick on your collar:
she carried a taser and a gun.

By then we were so used to each other
we used each other.
We kept using the familiar terms
even while meeting the others. Dear heart,
betrayal became you.

I was addicted to the lifestyle
we called home
though my hands trembled, my knees knocked together.
He called my name. I staggered at the tipping point.

All drugs sing the song of the end of pain.
This is what happens to humans
addicted to love:
they either kick the habit or accept
the price of long-term use.
You reached for me in the dark
as the fire died down, lit me
and drew me in
leaned to stir the embers
to see if any light was left.

My body ignited.

Another linguistic lesson.

L'amour qui brûle en moi. There is no such thing
as harm reduction.

Compersion

Trust the lovers to come up with jealousy's
opposite. Trust
us to fail at it. Compersion,
the feline softness of the word,
purring around your ankles, *yes*, I'll always
be happy for you, wherever you fuck
your happiness. *Trust me*, I said,
I'm going to the Polyamory Meet-n-Greet
I won't be back late. Room a clash of perfumes,
colognes musk patchouli deodorant cleavage
myriad men even the windows ran with steam
I could hardly breathe and not in a good way
in this jasmine greenhouse
taken hostage by bonobos it was an All-You-Can-Eat
buffet in a strip mall. Amid such excess
appetite flees.

I was an anthropologist
studying compersion rituals. Members
are addicted to variety, to complication
to drama. O who would you like
to play doctor with tonight? I left
with a dry mouth, with some numbers,
it must be said, in my pocket.

Compersion requires more talk
than seven average marriages.
How arousing.
None of them had children:
they had lovers instead.
I was a wallflower at the bus stop
on the route to rapture.
No, it was more than that:

despite precautions
love is not always preventable.

How many can we love?
What's the human limit?

You wanted me to be happy
even if I couldn't be happy
with you. For us all the wrong answers
in love's calculus. I threw the numbers out
on the SkyTrain home, though I thought
about leaving them on the seat
for strangers, for random compersion:
the purest kind of desire.

Once someone said when I left her
Why can't you love me? You're going to love someone.
Why not me? Don't speak. Any answer
is the wrong answer.
Jealousy, like everything else, is on a continuum
and like everything else, we're just average, you and I
though I miss the years we thought otherwise.

But I wanted compersion to work! Like communism,
it's an excellent theory. Share the love, the bread,
the pocket of coins. Share the bed, the house, the chores
the venereal diseases.
I ache for the beautiful theories
to be true—socialist, anarchist, libertarian—
Especially fidelity.
I came home late that night
to your quiet breathing alone in our bed.
I sat awake in the dark, yearning.
Watched you dreaming.

The Horses

All that terrible spring
when you were making up your mind
whether to leave me
I fought against it with everything
I had. I had nothing.
You had to break me like I used to watch,
from the back of my horse, the women break horses,
shifting their weight every time their mounts tried to escape,
turning the snaffle bit between their lips
so that they had only one view, so that their heads
turned and they had to follow, so that they finally
accepted exhaustion and stood, flanks wet with labour,
heaving, having surrendered.

In truth I was a wild horse that bolted
and when your boot caught in the stirrup
I dragged you over rough ground until you
were broken. Yes, that was me, that bucking spinning
animal, lashing out.

That was you at the same time,
the kind of woman who beats a horse
until her crop breaks, that was who we became
that was what
we didn't mean our bodies to do.

One day, just like that, a stranger came to town
and said *Let there be hurt*—
and it was Babylon.

Finally what bound us broke
and you fell clear of those battering hooves.
At last I lost my will to fight and stood in the harsh light

trembling all over, let my big head drop in the dust.
We stood in the centre of the pasture
just two animals breathing
and then one of us moved toward the other
and the other stepped cautiously forward.
We smelled one another, great heaving breaths
the smell was terror and old sweat
the smell was grass foam and sugar
the smell was new: you tossed your head,
I dipped my muzzle to your shoulder, nipped.
we wheeled, we ran together the wild darkening hills,
lowered our heads as the sun sank, drank the sky's milk.

Marry and Burn

After we drew blood
and recoiled, we looked at the great grave

of our life together, stepped back from the abyss.
Your kiss was blue lupine caught in a glacier.

We each envisioned the path not taken.
Darling, like the monarch butterfly

I cannot touch you
without brushing away your magic.

All I thought familiar
has been made mysterious by the almost-break

the near-vanishing. If this too is a mistake
know that love made me stay. No escape

from being wounded: the blessing.
And in the end? At best one alone to mourn

one to bury. Burn and marry.

Corona for Charlotte

I.

Now we can never leave this house
where the blind dog knows her way.
All dogs must die; a dog is not a spouse,
I know her death will come soon, yet still the noise

of her feet tick-tocking across the floor
her bright eyes expectant in the foyer
her long sigh as she curls by the door
and our slow walks formalize the day.

I brought her home when I was twenty-one
and everything seemed possible, but hard.
My lover moved out just as the dog moved in—
I planted white petunias in the yard.

I had only vague hopes of what would be.
I learned to live in quiet company.

II.

I learned to live in my own company
alone, but for my books, my pen, my dog.
Alone, but with a sense of *joie d'esprit*—
between myself and life, a dialogue!

I answered back to books, I wrote all night
through sultry Montreal's sticky July
and with her small black head upon my feet
the dog dreamed big. When it was time to play

she'd prance and spin, she'd bring the leash and howl.
I'd put aside my books and we would walk
to bright *café-terraces* where dogs were allowed.
And in the evenings she'd listen while I'd talk.

Lovers came and went, but not the mutt.
We stayed together. I named her Charlotte.

III.

She knew *sit* and *stay*. I named her Charlotte.
When I moved to Japan, she came with me
The children at the school smiled when she'd visit.
In my house by the river I'd sit with tea,

trace characters till they spoke nouns and vowels.
We'd walk down by the river, all alone
among the fishermen and the flowering willows
while sensible Japanese housewives stayed in town.

We'd go without umbrellas in the rain!
It was easy to be shocking in that place.
She'd drowse on tatami, then creep to my futon.
I snuck her on the train in a carry case.

And when my friend, at twenty, died in her sleep,
I walked into the river. She barked when I went too deep.

IV.

She'd bring me back when I went too far or deep.
She'd run through drifts of snow in Parc la Fontaine.
My lover and I found a flat and lived on the cheap
and the dog slept on our bedspread in the sun.

Those were delicious years, just me and *ma blonde*
and the dog that was mine became the dog that was ours.
I'd walk her to medical school as the morning dawned
and pick her up sick with fatigue after twenty-four hours.

When our firstborn came, we didn't have love or time.
We moved the dog to a basket with a towel.
When the others were born, she'd already grown resigned.
If she approached while I was nursing, I would growl.

She's seventeen. I'm middle-aged. She's can't see.
Last night she shook and cried out in agony.

V.

Last night she shook and cried out in agony.
Today I carry her outside to the warm grass.
She lifts her vacant head and smells the sea.
I get a shovel. For now her pain has passed.

Dig past the black loam to the sand hard as cement.
Today her pain has passed. How do we make the call
and say this is the day her death was meant
to be? A blister breaks my palm. She walks into the wall

and turns and walks into the fence, panting,
asking nothing. Once she barfed a condom on the rug
chewed out the crotches of used panties
ate a tampon that made her terribly plugged.

She always ate too much. She once got lost, then found.
We'll pick a day, and bury her in the ground.

VI.

We'll pick a day and bury her in the ground,
but the grave stands open under the lilac tree.
I carried her in just as the rain came down,
and the children came and asked if she would die

and *ma blonde* said, yes, we would put her down,
and we'd be with her the whole time, we'd help her die.
We'd push the needle and hold her until she was gone,
and the children looked at us with serious eyes.

The heart-stopping liquid went in and her breath went out.
I know she's just a dog. I know it's practice.
I kept my hands on her until she was not.
For days the baby calls her, dragging around the leash.

When the pain is gone, there's silence.
Now we can never leave this house.

Good Measure

We left this house, the dog, the garden.
We broke the vows, the hearth, the marriage.
We left behind for good measure
dust, debt, sediment. Left the ash,
the keys, cushions to the futon
 in the crawl space. A cracked tank
emptied of fish. We left
discards at the curb. Left the fights
the separate beds, the separate loves, the place
our daughter learned to walk
and run.

We left this house. We left
the built-in vacuum, the neighbor's leaf blower
a man who edged his lawn with scissors. We left
the picket fence, white lilac. Left
a double-wide garage, a stack of bricks
fire with a switch left off.
 The years left lines upon our face.

Each false start, ash of the dog under bleeding hearts.
Poppies, orange and gold. A stack of textbooks.
Those years blew through us. You took a hit of sadness
then blew smoke in my mouth. I held it in
until I saw stars.

There was a fire, dog's grit and bone, cold tea
in a cold mug, gold ring returned.
We left a forwarding address
pencil marks in the doorframe:
the height they were at different times
though we'd stopped growing long since.

Tooth

The need roughens in me to have love. The way the paper has
tooth.

—Lynn Strongin

You roughened the need in me
the way paper has tooth
the way metal has rust
the way a song has bass
the way silk has warp and weft
to have love.

You silkened the need in me
the way a thistle has silk
the way a baby breaks teeth
the way chilled milk lifts cream
the way the sun pinks a berry
the way the moon silks the sea
to be loved.

I held a need in me
the way the match holds sulfur
the way the lamp holds kerosene
the way the eyes draw light
the way the tree calls lightning
and you lit it and left.

The need grew in me
the way yeast grows bread
the way a scream grows the chest
the way a baby grows the passage
the way a cut grows blood
the way a secret grows trust
the way a burn grows blisters—
till it burst.

A new path travelled in me
the way a ship travels the ocean
the way cattle travel trails
the way needles travel veins
the way robbers travel a highway
the way collections travel the church
the way rations travel to refugees—
and I stepped out.

But you came back—
the way a ring slips back on a finger
the way the cat turns in the window
the way an army returns with a truce

and as my abandoned wish came true
the need roughened in me to choose.

There was the path or the hearth
the heart or the hurt
the lie or the lyre
a new start or a new stillness.
There were the years or the yearning
the known or the unknowing.
There was the door or the wind—
and the wind, the wind had teeth.

I stood in that wild wind, blown and undecided
as Lot's wife. I looked down that path in the roughened
dark, then looked back at you, pouring salt
in the fire. I stood in the wind, holding it all
in hand, weighing it. But you were not Lot,
we were not lost, we had traversed
flood and storm, you brought the cold in,
I carried fire on my back, we had come to the end

of the odyssey, swept up the debris.
Blown I came in roughened by love
and you met me with your mouth.

II.

Legends

Only Fire: An Inventory

The first time you dream in French
the way the words come *doucement, sans
hésitation*, as though you belong to that language.

When she came home again, and hope burst
the casks of iron girding your chest. Her eyes:
old answers, new questions. Gold that stays.

Stroking the old dog as the needle goes in,
lolls her tongue. Tears spatter her coat:
rain on a dusty road.

Mulberries. Pinworms.
Killing dinner. The long
work of gutting rabbits. How hard the stretched hide.

Swimming naked in a warm pond
in a cold rain with a woman your mother asked
to watch you. Furious joy.

Waking up between him and her in the stained sheets
of their house. Unwrapping their legs from the gift you were.
Their eyes, meeting yours: each holding a different story.

Hers blurred by regret, and his,
a secret he would squander.
You, leaving, took from someone's tree

figs so ripe they split their skins,
because you never could resist stolen sweetness.
The grit of the bones of a dead friend in a can of ash

you fling off the boat. How he puffs back, blinds you,
clogs your throat.
Eat me, says his soul, and you do.

Orgasm. The ocean. Snow. The skin of a manta ray.
The skin of a dolphin. The skin of a newborn.
Northern lights.

Fresh durian. Burying grandmother. The week after, boxing
her high heels. The red ones with the buckles.
Trying to force your feet in.
The bear crossing your path, the two cubs also.
All your life you've been afraid of bears until just that moment.
There is no "you." Only bears. Only fire.

Not death, but the moment just after.

Living on Islands I

It is hard for the dying to leave us.
We make it hard for them. So they wait
for us to step outside before they cut
the cord. So the baby
in the cabin, lungs full of staph
who had been fighting the infection
for long nights and days
waited until his mother went out
to chop firewood before he sighed
and stilled. How can I forget her
running across the wet pasture
with his body in her arms
as though my mother were a witch
who could bring back the dead?
I picked the thick white lilies from our garden
for his grave but was not permitted to the place
where the mourners gathered. Instead I waited
in the silent house, unfolded
the image of his mother
with her hair wild as the wind
and the weight of him in her arms
a stone, a feather, a sunflower
as my mother rose to meet her
or what I have imagined, the map of memory
creased and softened
like a star repeating its trajectory into the sea
the girl who could never forget
and the father who did not yet know
coming up the gravel driveway
with a shovel over his shoulder
whistling, kicking the mud off his boots
before he opened the door.

Living on Islands II (Rune of the Fatherland)

After Marilyn Hacker's Rune of the Finland Woman

He could turn back the ship when I slipped to sea.
He could captain a schooner with a drunken crew.
He could gaff a rockfish with a double blow.
He could haul me on deck with a roughened towel.

He could pull a body from a grasping lake.
He could carry a drowned girl to her mother's arms.
He could hack the mold from a stale cake.
He could fence a pasture with posts and barbs.

He could steam the ribs of a newborn boat.
He could build his lover a house of cedar.
He could build his daughter a dragon cradle.
He could sever the tongue of a still-warm cow.

He could bottlefeed a lamb with beaten milk.
He could kill a dog with a strangling embrace.
He could climb a mountain in an afternoon.
He could take a ship to Jerusalem.

He could shoot a bullseye from a hundred yards.
He could pull six arrows from a bed of straw.
He could father two children in different beds.
He could join the army and break the law.

He could row a dory through a midnight storm.
He could carry a man with a broken back.
He could chop six trees to a winter stack.
He could leave the island in a rusted truck.

He could man a train down a coal-black track.
He could flood a mine with a hardhat light.
He could crack a geode for a birthday gift.
He could kill a buck deer with a single shot.

He could wash with soap in a winter lake.
He could whitewash a loss with a magic trick.
He could stitch a sail with a hand-held awl.
He could hide a matzo in an unseen spot.

He could cross a threshold with a sudden threat.
He could thresh a harvest with a horse-drawn cart.
He could splint the bent leg of a biting hawk.
He could haul a halibut to a leaky boat.

He could eat a horse when the money ran out.
He could borrow the boots from a dead man's feet.
He could drink fresh cream from a pail of milk.
He could turn back the ship when I slipped to sea.

Living on Islands III

As the island's only doctor
She had priority on the party line.
When a woman in labour needed her
she drove island roads double time.

That night I was wide awake—
she'd stoked the fire, boiled water
—though often I slept or looked at books.
The woman panted, it sounded like laughter.

I watched from a crouch on the ground
as she arched and pushed.
She screamed as the baby crowned
and in that shitmeat air I retched.

My mother unwrapped the blue package, worked the knot,
scrubbed the chest as if rubbing out a stain.
The baby in her hand hung mute.
The woman twisted and screamed again

and my mother pushed a bowl in my direction,
shoved me between the high knees,
yelled *Hang on!*—
as the placenta was born

and the baby bubbled a scream,
and the mother's blood dripped on the wood,
and my mother stitched a black seam,
stripped the bed

then cleaned my blood-dried hands,
her face tight with exhaustion. All night
she kept kerosene lamplight vigil as I slept in her coat,
and in me the poem began its distillation, its slow symbiotic gestation.

Sunflowers

Ruby-throated rufous dash-darting,
deep-throating red-flowering currant, sip-slipping
to dally with dahlias. O red rover, come hover
come hither, quick as a cat's leap swipes jewels
from air.

Mother, I knew you best
in your garden, scattering sunflowers for the warblers,
your hands broad
and more useful than trowels,
       your hands
that an old boyfriend called
the ugliest hands I've ever seen on a woman.
Hands that feed sugar to hummingbirds,
hands that delivered, hands
that called the time of death.

Mother, where did you go?

Pull a single stitch. Pull and wind and order.
Your mad sadness is a hundred skeins of yarn
knotted in the roots at the bottom of the cellar.
Which of us has come unravelled?

Remember that afternoon
of living gold, that swarm of bees clustered
in the alder in your yard?   Each drop poured
    risen to a tree
turned treasure chest, gold
      that paused to rest.
Honey to mitigate the sting
      of what can't be said.
    Before the first star

the beekeeper came in his space suit.
                  So gold subsides to gold:
bees taken away as the moon appeared
fragile as a petal against the late blue.

Wild, you were wild and no one could hold you.
Only the birds ate at your table.
Only the moon was your good daughter.

Bees

The farmer asked me to host a hive
　　　and I said yes thinking honey,
　　　　　　without the sting, thinking

do your small
　　　part and let the bees do theirs.
　　　　　　The hive was a box of many rooms

hot with life.
　　　It throbbed under its tin roof
　　　　　　All summer their flight path

hung its line of light across the deck.
　　　Those gold cells swam to the door
　　　　　　of the hive, dusted with lust from blossom.

If a wasp dared come, they were ready
　　　to kamikaze down, force the intruder out
　　　　　　in a buzz-tussle to the death. I crouched.

I watched the stinger torn from the bee's body
　　　　　　trailing cream. Even in death, bees are never lonely.
　　　　　　　　　The hive is myriad.

The hive is more than the bees.
　　　Sometimes I stood close to vibrate with them,
　　　　　　drone of sun, pleasure of reaching beyond the limited

human. O stamen, pistil, I let them tangle in my hair
　　　I hung up their flight path. Then came the virus,
　　　　　　and then the wasps. There was no keeping them out.

I crushed a few invaders, before I stopped,
       stupid human, helpless as any God
           before the laws of relativity.

The farmer and I could barely look at each other
       and the leaves fell and brought winter.
           But can we try again? I begged, like a woman

who wakes to a bed of blood, *can we try again?*
       The serious farmer said, *Of course.* The struggle
           is all that keeps me here, in this plague time

where bees drop, the hive is cold, a few hornets
       drift, a virus drifts, pesticides drift over lawns
           lush as death, fields of strawberries so poisoned

and perfect one bite brings the sleep
       of a hundred years. Can we try again?

Hive Mind

The hive is sick. Several global wars
are burning. I am building a wailing wall
around my house. It is made of wax.
The hive is infected, but the tree is strong.

The tree is sick. Several viruses have infected
the tree. The hive is dead. I have shrouded
all the mirrors in my house. Would you like tea
with lemon and honey? Let me rend your garments.
The tree is infected, but the forest is manifold.

The forest is sick. Several companies have harvested
the crop. I have said Kaddish for arbutus,
cedar and fir. Who doesn't prefer
urban comfort? The mountain is barren,
but there are many mountains.

The weather is sick. Hot and cold flushes, tsunami
and snow, flood and storm. O hivemind
enter the mind palace, stop your ears with wax
to keep the news out. That constant buzzing.
Hivemind, I am stung all over
a burn so great it is ice at fire's heart.
I swell until my throat closes.

Let me live as a tree does
holding song and honey, lightning
and the gold drops of bees
coming in from the rain.
Let me learn to eat light.

Growing Pains

Tonight I feel the loneliness
of being cisgender.

I have no boy inside me.
It's been years, if ever.

Some are kissed in their cradles
by the two faces of Janus,
god of transitions
god of war. They barely survive that kiss,

forevermore hold both kinds of joy,
and the twelve kinds of pain.

The rest of us, unkissed,
breathe the ordinary lullaby.
We live one kind of lonely.

Golden Age

This one is for the girls
who got themselves to the party
and didn't get home, girls
who got drunk like angels—glimmering,
disappearing—then woke up under a towel
in a strange hotel. This is the glass of words to toast
your bad choices, the wink of a boy
tonguing your navel. Unconscious-
ly your own desire to be touched
was a claim you couldn't stake, a willow
that needed water. This is the blame you've birthed,
cradled and nursed, blame that won't leave home
because you didn't bite, didn't sit up, you just
closed your eyes and drifted on a sad river of burning
alcohol. This is for all the passive girls, the ones who sucked off
popular boys, the ones who half wanted to be wanted,
half wanted to die. To die a little death
as you did then, when you came to school
and the rumour was he'd fucked you with the handle
of a broom while you were floating down
the Ganges, the Nile, the Fraser, the Thames.
Gone: was it true or wasn't it? There was no pain,
it was a lie, it was a myth. This is for you,
bitch, snatch of gossip in the hall,
twist of hair, sucker punch. This is for me, too:
girl of the skinned knees who couldn't name the names
of those who'd passed through her body.
This is for leaving school, or staying. For the dangerous
damaged pack we make, the way we smell blood
where other girls smell roses. Sinister sorority!
Who knew that one day we would consider
ourselves lucky to have been raped
in the golden age of rape, before violation

was caught on an iPhone: posted, reposted. Look!
A close-up on sleeping beauty digitally defiled
and then digitally defiled. What poisoned apple
blocks her throat from screaming? Boots jostle. Time fucks
faster now. Featherweight, angelweight, song of floating
above the below. Blow and she's still still: moth dust, shimmer.
Unbuckle your belt, her eyelids. She can't move away,
can't change schools. Even dead, there is
no escape. Link it. Click like. It takes three thousand views
in three hours to make a myth.

Confusion

Language is the hardest game.
We planned a family like writing an outline
for a novel. We were brand new though not innocent.
Confucius says, *If language is not correct*
then what is said is not what is meant, then what must be done
remains undone. So much remains to be undone
which is why I am not a language poet I am afraid:
how can I make it plain?
I mean I spend my days cleaning up messes not making them.
I cut off crusts. Who trusts a reader's intentions
alone with an underage text in a parking garage?
Who is that guy you were
talking about—Confusion? asks my daughter.
It's easy to be puzzle-dazzled. And so she's confused
Bellingham with Bethlehem, stewardess with uterus,
and that kind of cancer that razzled a friend's husband?
She calls it prostitute cancer.
Cipher of my body, little daughter, sons
following mothers' footsteps in a family for which
language is the hardest game. Remember the time
when our wee son came running in
to shout, *Mama Isa, guess what? Mama Rach*
is a lesbian! Laugh, O! Laugh at the unwitting comedian.
He stood there smiling in confucius
wondering what joke rumbled
beyond the beyond the years.
We are the clan no language has words for
the science-forged tribe we created in a dream.
She is just the kind of man I meant to marry,
I am her unspeakable until whensoever.

Negotiation

I was thinking in the range of eighty thousand.
Those numbers sound reasonable to me.
Actually more like a hundred thousand.

Those numbers don't scare me.
A German estimate numbers the galaxies at 500 billion.
Those numbers sound reasonable to me.

The earth grows more crowded as we grow lonelier.
The average family is now one and a half people.
Those numbers don't scare me.

A hundred and fifty species go extinct every day.
You don't know what you've got until it burns.
Those numbers sound reasonable to me.

Mao claimed 45 million, Hitler 11 million, Stalin 10 to 20 million
which is not as precise as we might wish. One sun, one moon.
Those numbers don't scare me.

The gods claim their respective holocausts. Negotiations stall
and it keeps getting hotter. Ours is the faith known as *self-medicating*.
Those numbers sound reasonable to me.
Those numbers don't scare me.

The Introduction

At the play about evil—
the way the land was stolen,
families broken apart, sent to camps—
my children sit, open-mouthed.
It is time, we have decided
to introduce them to evil, as my grandmother
took me to walk with her friends, those battered
blue-blotched men who showed me the numbers
on their rope-thin arms, and laughed to have cheated death
found themselves washed up in Coral
Gables eating my grandmother's kugel
though at night the darkness pressed on me
thick with crocodiles, Nazi hunters, survivors
who slit matchsticks in two to have twice as much fire.

The play about evil is described by critics as universal.
There are songs and we can only protect them
for so long without damaging them.

In the car, after, the boys watch cars go by,
leaning against the seat as though waking from a deep sleep,
but the girl says, *I would run so fast, they could never catch me.*
They would catch you, says her brother.
Then I would cut the fence at night and run into the mountains.
They would shoot you, says her brother without mercy,
and she bursts into fury, pounding her fists
against the seat, exploding a rainstorm of tears.
They would NOT shoot me! she screams.
I would kill them first! She rejects her introduction
to evil, spits it out, fights the lesson, as she spat
out her first strained peas, refused what we thought
was good for her, would make her strong.

Serious

The problem was love, or perhaps the problem was trust.
The problem was in each of us. And it was serious.

The problem was the kind of love we sought,
the kind that demands a price so pitiless—

better to lock the door and cry alone.
Even the abortion, even the faceless men oblivious

by the bonfire's glorious burn could not
make us say it. Girl, we were fucked. I'm delirious.

Now, at midpoint, everything hangs in the balance:
marriage, friendship, our willingness to greet the morning. Hey, Genius,

you with your prescription addiction, devious, mysterious,
thrown onto glass by that latest crash. Seriously,

why can't we bear being loved, that brutal vulnerability? It burns.
My limp, our scars, your body's notorious

affinity for pain. You write, *Friend, life is so sad. I think
I will be ready to let it go when it is time.* Seer

who sees through all of us: don't be my star
who goes nova, don't be my myth of a friend. See her?

That's the child you were when your parents unsealed their vows
and took up their lies. When there isn't a clear escape, sear

of one loss bleeding into another, you were the only one
I could call. Fall or ascend, we both have glorious

troubles, but at least you are not afraid
of telling me the truth, that precarious

reckoning. Another thing: I'm still glad I broke
down your door that year years ago, and sat with fearless

you on your couch, bleeding that trace of union
out, not wanting to be witnessed in your pain, but seriously

it was better you weren't alone: forgive me. Or don't.
Isn't it curious? You saved my life. And I was furious.

Nitpicking

When you imagined children, you pictured
new teeth, dimples, lace socks, budding
vocabulary. Not notes sent home
that lice have been found again
in Divisions 2, 3, 6, 8, 9 and 10,
with instructions on how to kill them.
No use crying into unwashed laundry.
Line them up, lollipops for silence,
small payment for the violence of the fanged comb
whose metal teeth scrape white scalps raw.
Wipe the sweat of irritation from your eyes. Force
patience. There are as many ways a mother can fail
as nits on a child's soft head.

Each depends upon
your careful hands, glazed with mist
from a spray bottle's pulse. Time is six fine hairs
cleaned and pinned. Now hush, now
lean in. Yawn. Yawn again.
Nits are stars in a sky
of midnight's mane.

A tiny crab travels down your son's nape—
you smash it between the nails
of your thumbs. You are the groom upon whom
they must depend. Calm your hands.
Love is made manifest in the lousy tasks, the ones
no one wants. Settle into the primal
grooming ritual. Unknot the brambles.

Kneel here, as if in prayer, scraping nits from their hair.

The Prayer

In the morning I prayed the prayer of thanks
for having not been made a man.
I prayed the prayer of the unbeliever
which required that I bite the hand that feeds me.
It was the morning of the first day. I said Kaddish
for the dead and the undead. Which is to say
living. Which is to say *my own hand*, owned
by mine teeth. How I prayed for belief!
It was the evening of the first day
and I prayed the prayer of thanks
for having been made to bleed.

I lacked the genetic code for piousness.
It was the second day. What do you know? Sunrise!
I prayed the prayer of thanks for having not been made
a Christian. Which is to say *known entity*.
It was a long day, the second day. No moon.
I prayed in bed with you for the second
coming. I took the Lord's name in vain.
Which is to say I spake it in passion.
Which is to say I linked my body to the holy war
of creation. Whom shall forgive whom?

The third day was a dawn of rain.
All day white mushrooms bloomed in the wet leaves.
My grief was like unto the fungus spreading leagues underground
but all that emerged were those white fingers pressing
through the grave of earth. *Let there be sleep*, you said
and I slept.

The fourth day was an eclipse in the temple.
I prayed on my knees to the gold circlet of darkness
that had once been the sun. I prayed in the four directions

and burned the four sacrificial hearts, read the ash
for clues. As the smoke rose
the waters rose in the four directions.
No prayer could cool that benediction of heat
and I believed, at least, in fire.

It was the morning of the fifth day
and I prayed the prayer of thanks for having not been born
a lamb. As we ate you wiped my bloodied lips with linen.
We lifted our goblets of light and smashed them on the tabernacle.
Which is to say we prayed the prayer of those who have drunk
to abandon themselves. Which is to say we became unrecognizable
to each other. Which is to say I'm sorry I was unfaithful
though I remember little of the act. Your body was a shrine
but I went through the wrong gate.

We were glad for the sixth day.
We were hungover with effort and joy. Which is to say
we prayed the prayer of children on a treasure hunt.
I said the words of thanks to God for not having made me gold.
Night was a relief. I stared through the darkness
at the domes of mosques.

On the seventh day we could not rest. You paced the dawn.
I sang the scream of beaten women. You wailed at the wall. I kissed
the bronze knife of the Goddess. You ripped the sacred garments.
I served the breasts and miracles
on a platter of relics. You lit the joss sticks
and copied the sutras by hand.
I plucked the eyes from the vine
caught the stones in my mouth. I said the prayer
of thanks for not having to be reborn. Which
is to say Ash. Which is to say Amen.

Blessing Ivy's Eyes

When a friend asks me to meet her
in the middle of the afternoon
on the last day the Tibetan monks
will be in the Chinese gardens,
pouring their sand mandalas' final patterns
on the eighth day of the seventh month
I do not refuse.

My marriage is imploding and her vision is moving
into the valley of the shadow, but why speak
of such things when you can't change fate? My throat
is full of unshed tears, the sky is full of rain,

her eyes are thick with clouds. She traces Chinese characters
onto sheets of paper with a brush as thick
as a finger, and I teach her the English phrase
mind's eye, the place where she can still see her
complicated alphabet, her husband's hands.
From her I learn that blindness
is a white sheet full of holes
hung across the cherry trees
and she can only see through the holes, but the wind
is blowing, petals are tossed, the whole sky
is filled with dazzling light, not darkness,
which comforts me.

Oh the purity of the blind face listening, the value of friends
who walk arm in arm, speaking not of the damage
that has befallen them. Bitter tea poured out to us,
we cup the warmth, I describe the
rain dimpling the koi ponds outside, the golden lotus
blooming with needles of rain, addicts' needles
drifting to rock bottom.

My friend who walks into walls
and makes a joke of it. My friend who lets me lean on her arm
and pretend I'm guiding her: how much it means to you
to be here, who spent your childhood in an umbrella factory,
working the small stitch in dim light, though that's not why
your eyes broke. You left your country, your language,
and now you'll leave the culture of the visible world.

My friend: the monks clamber onto their stools,
cross their burgundy robes and tap the metal funnels to pour
the blue sand against the white sand,
and you can't see the subtle creation.
In four hours, they'll destroy everything,
stirring with rough hands,
wild boys again.

Hold on to nothing: that's the lesson.
Build with deliberate care the object of great beauty, then tear
it down yourself. Do not cling.
The abbot with earlobes
plump as dumplings smiles at us
as you buy the prayer bowls, and I ask him to bless
your eyes. Gently, he cups your face close to his, blows
soft breath into each lid, prays. You hold still as a girl
waiting for a sliver to be pulled, your hand open
in mine. My eyes fill
with something we might call pain.
The next week, your doctor writes the order for your cane.

City of Myth

I drove through Innisfail.
Alberta stretched out before me bleak as a marriage
where words for pleasure have been forgotten.
I was the stranger who came to town
and I courted the myth.

For auld lang syne I wept in my sleeve
I sojourned the myth. I confess I was weary.
Lowther was "weary of atrocities" and then she was killed.
Her husband did it. I read *wary*.
I was my own wife, pyrrhic, myrrh'd.
I anthologized poems only by murdered Canadians.
It was gender-neutral, racially diverse.
It was a residential school in winter
land of the silver birch, home of the child starved.
Wash your mouth with ash
and lye, true north proud and free.

I was simply sad, though sentiment
is myth and not to be counted.

I dreamed now I've written this poem
I can be done with poetry.
I turned on my pillow sobbing tears of gratitude
now I could return to real life:
the myth
of the good mother.

I had the myth-fortune of marriage
to a maiden. I was myth-
taken about most everything.
No use crying over spilled myth.

I am the first born in this country.
My father lit his passport but it didn't burn well.
Amerika was a curse and a measuring stick,
a threat and a plan.
Here, they said, is where you will be
transplanted. They made me,
birthed me, buried me, watered me well,
uprooted me, myth-tutored me,
then returned to their own country.
The myth was lost in migration.

When Harper said, "We have no history
of colonialism," clearly he myth-spoke,
he myth-calculated, we myth-voted.
I feel naked without the myth.
The myth was good for my self-esteem.

Myth, come back!

The myth was I could write my own myth
pull it from the teeth
of the air, mouth of sky
make it new. I sewed the myth
onto my backpack when I travelled
trident red leaf.

Grove of silver birches around a mass grave
behind the remains of a church school.
It's a mote that blinds
a sliver of ice the moist tongue of a priest
the weight of snow.

The myth was blue as our clean
Canadian icebergs, calved
from the mother's body, submerged.

This year the myth shifted
tectonically. Our home and native land.
We went quietly to the healing ceremony
and stood to the side as the crowd testified,
wept, testified. Elders
fanned tobacco on my children
over my body, without discrimination
but what stung my eyes was the myth.

III.

Addictions

City of Addiction

Welcome to the city of addiction.
Welcome to hell. This city's natural beauty
is moist as a scallop's lung, mountains melting
into ocean, ocean rising to meet real estate.
Those trees, so dark, so manly.
Hell serves free sandwiches
if you line up early. The lineups
shuffle and stagger around corners.
Hell is an alley where they found her body
and her body. My brother missed her
by an hour. An hour! There are slices
of processed cheese, rolls, free coffee.
The city of addiction has a life expectancy
of thirty-five. Pass the laughter yoga
class, shuffle off this morning's tremor
light curdled on the horizon
branches pulling in sap thick as opium
green as wine. In this city, your breath hangs
like plum blossom in the cold light
and everywhere is twelve steps
from water. After the memorial
wake to fresh astonishment
at outliving those who left. In the city
of addiction, nothing is personal.
Left through the alley, off the balcony, over the bridge
on the floor between bedroom and bathroom
overdosed on their own choked blood.
City of rats and saxophones
where the tail hair of horses is pulled
across strings to make an audience
feel what it has lost.
Instrument held so close
it scars the neck.

This city. Other cities.
Checked out without paying.
Took leave without saying goodbye.

The Test

I had to write in loops with a penny balanced
on the back of my hand. I wrote my name,
copied out cursive text. I had to ride
my horse around the ring holding a glass of champagne.
I had to roll into a canter. I was told to stride
with a dictionary on my head as if there were
a string between me and God. I
had to carry an egg in a spoon
and trot my mare, who was in heat, around a dusty ring.
I had to bring an egg home and call it my child.
I had to love without hope of profit.
I had to walk behind a pony with an alder switch.
I had to wash the pus from my baby's clogged eyes.
I had to reach past the accusations to name the fear.
The test was a balancing act. There were
no retakes. The test was true or false.
The test was whether I could own the harm
and make amends. I had to feed winter ducks
the crusts from outstretched fingers.
I had to inject myself in a pinch of skin.
I had to waterboard the dog. I mean wash her
in the sink. I had to learn to ask for help.
I mean speak the words out loud with my mouth:
Please help me. The test was multiple choice
so all other answers were wrong.
The test was whether you were your addiction
or your addiction simply tested you. The test was
an open bottle of wine and two clean glasses.
Behind one door was the rest of your life, behind the other
your death and there was no third door.

The Lifestyle

At this point it is clear as a shot
of vodka: I'm addicted to life. My heart
is addicted to the body electric hip hop
my lungs are addicted to the rush
of air they pull from the pipe of my throat
twelve times a minute. None of us
is looking forward to withdrawal
which I've heard takes every ounce
of will just to surrender. I'm not ready
to give up the lifestyle. Walking uphill
the white Pacific shrouded in mist
pines bleeding their Japanese ink,
carrying within me
my addiction to breath
also the seed of my own death
in clouds of inspiration
each step on the path.

When it comes, pervious lungs, enjoy the last
exhalation and know, *that was a job well and truly done.*
Heart, put down your four hammers and let the wild blood
still. Hair, grow toward the light a little longer
but eyes, dream of the sea nudging the land
like a lover presses against the beloved in midnight's bed
asking without speaking for bliss.
Last breath: the sea, yes, but also freshly turned earth
in a spring garden, hot concrete poured
in the pedestrian street. O ears
thrum and hush, and hands, bide a while
as withdrawal sets in, the shaking stops
and the door opens to the end
we're fixing for. As one body we rush it
push into the quiet.

Light of Addiction

Darkling I listen; and, for many a time
I have been half in love with easeful Death,
Call'd him soft names in many a mused rhyme,
To take into the air my quiet breath . . .

                                        —Keats, "Ode to a Nightingale"

Let me make light of addiction.
Let us understand each other. I who have
paid with the pact of my childhood. I
who have passed on the debt unto the seventh
generation. Let me make of addiction, light:
Lightling I sing, liebe, let me lift you lightly
away from oblivion, let me be unbenumbed,
awake in what happens with all my senses,
to exist until I can face it, even broken
among the rising seas
and the dying bees, even if you, like the others gone,
choose easeful death with his soft names,
his smother-cloak. Love you through it.
Love you until you are here no longer
to be loved, as I have loved before you each of
the twelve apostles of addiction, their edges,
their exhalations, their sincere lies, their observations.
Lightling let me love you not as you love yourself
until you feel the burn of it as you fight
in the coil of addiction. Serenity is a stream
running backward to the mouth of a mountain.
I am halfway between you and a dark place.
I lack the wisdom to know the difference
between where my body stops and yours begins.
Maybe I can't keep you, maybe it won't be enough,
but I will watch you until the sponge of the sky
has been wrung of the last drops
of light, until the stars go out I will never turn away.

79

Personal Inventory: Wine to Wine Lover

Darling, it's time to put the *shun*
back in addiction. Do as I say,
not as I sashay. Do as I do re mi.
Kiss me, twirl me: I'll tell you just what
you should say to be the life of the party.
Let's shun reality for numb fun, baby.
Why habituate to unadulterated life? Decant me,
let me fill your throat.

Unbearable to live without God, you say
without fur and with free will—
though you have left your hearth
and tried to leave me,
have wandered naked,
husked, silken, threshed.
There's no way back to belief.
It's me or the empty vessel,
the unbroken joyless horizon
of abstinence. But we both know that.
Those grapes, sweetheart,
have been picked. Come to bed.
Let me stain you.

I don't judge. I spread for anyone. I'm laid back.
You squeezed me into what you needed
and I just laughed, poured myself over you.

God says sorry for casting you
from the garden. Didn't know gardening was
therapeutic. Didn't know how much
you needed me. It was never the snake.
It was the fruit of the vine
that led Cain, that lead each of you

to knowledge of oblivion.
Thou shalt not numb
but God didn't realize
this would be such a big deal.

So anyway you can come back: the figs are bursting
their fine blue butts on the tree. God says
poem is mope spelled backward.
I know your will wavers. I love you anyway.
I am loyal to the death.

Shall we dance? Get up and dance.
Twelve Steps. Bed to Fridge.
Load the Boat.
All Around Your Left Hand Lady.
I've a little tune for you:

Nothing in the Left Hand
Nothing in the Right
I Knotted up My Kerchief
And Blotted Out the Night

Corkscrew. Explode the Wave.
My tongue in your ear.
I'm always thirsty.

Allemande Left, Allemande Thar
Inebriation's salubrious Star
Shining in my Upper Room
I Kissed the Rosy Cheek—of doom.

Twelve steps: shall we dance?

Hydrocodone: Help Wanted

The successful candidate will thrive
in the fast-paced dynamic environment
of this well-appointed private home.
Must have minimum three years'
experience. Must possess excellent oral
and interpersonal skills and be flexible
as to modes of consumption. Must be able
to maintain ironclad integrity of confidential
information. Ability to work evenings and weekends
unsupervised a requirement. Some
travel, some shift work, some rough
treatment. May be knocked down
with wine or swallowed dry.
May be thrown in the trash,
then picked out with tweezers.
We offer comprehensive benefits,
including but not limited to
extended prescription insurance,
complete access to the unmarked body
and bright tattered mind,
exciting possibilities for expansion.

Harm Reduction

Try something else then. Try sex.
What you need is just a different way to burn.
Marry me if you must. Or just
use my body for a night to wipe your lust
and addiction on. Go ahead: I'm civic
minded. There's more than one way to thread
a needle. Have me in an alley
for old time's sake. Have me in the truck
down by the lake where your skin tastes like smoke
and beer. Have me like a girl or a boy.
Eye to eye we go somewhere together
that is not here, somewhere that might cure.
You can disappear in me
if you close your eyes. We'll travel linked like trains
in a dark tunnel. Hold me down if you must.
Remember sleeping on trains?
That steady rumble, promise
of arrival. How everything tore past,
red poppies, dappled cows, how little we slept
in that rocking sleeping berth.
What was one night with you worth?
Charm me, then cut the charm.
Harm me, then reduce the harm.

Sublimation

Okay, not sex. Fine.
The little death didn't do it for you—
briefly out
in someone else's arms, quiet sleep after.
Rather, you couldn't get enough
and then you could. It was too safe
to get off, that latexed high. You couldn't make it new.
I understand. We are all withdrawn
here in the city of addiction.
But your choices are not
infinite, and you cannot live
without having to choose.

If not oblivion, what then?
What one thing will you do
until it burns? Here is a rope,
a cliff. Here is a casino, a credit card.
Here is a lottery ticket. Here are your famished ghosts.

Maybe it's words you crave
to describe the nature
of everything broken. First sniff
of free verse, free based, and yes,
you want to say *I do* forever.
Maybe it's muse, music
or the peace of being ritually cuffed, whipped
without a safe word, without consent.
It's exactly like sex without the sex.

      Hurt to numb
hit the pause button on reality.

Be a good citizen. Choose

a benign addiction.
Kettlebells, hot yoga, the downward dog
of middle age affairs, flesh melting
on the bone. Bring your work home
and lock the door. Morning after morning
on a treadmill going nowhere.
Substitute gluten, methadone. Substitute God.
I was sure I could love you hard enough
to free your will.

Rock Bottom

for Masarah

I sank to the lowest point
and now I drift a little.
It's peaceful here, facedown
in darkness. The weight of so much water
is better than any drug: I'm finally numb.

Far above me a ray of light
pierces the green sky. Kelp grooves
on the tidal pull. The gods have taken everything
but my pain: that I am allowed to keep.
Lovely scuttling crabs cross my waterlogged toes,
sea stars inch through their day.

      I am unbecoming human:
                   what a relief.

God drops disco: a bait ball
of blue jack mackerel
tornado their mass of silver,
scatter into knives,
ribbon my nether heaven.

Fine: I went down.
I dived into the wreck,
refused oxygen.
All I could not change
weighed me down. It just kept getting hotter.

Rock bottom.

      I am almost out of air.

Bubbles rise to another world, another war.
I am the latest refusenik. Whether
by cowardice or courage
I cannot be reconciled.

You ask me to live unsheltered, unskinned
from the daily drama. No tools of numbness,
no checking out.

You ask me in twelve steps
to speak, to make human

contact. I caught fire. A measure of alcohol
only the ocean's chill blanket could quench.

The first step: power
outage. Look, down here
I am safe from tides and weather
under the weight of tons of water.
Here are all my treasures, gold coins
swallowed by whales, shipwrecked pearls, bride price:
proof of my value. If I come back
I will not be whole. *Amen*. If I beat
my way to surface light
      Amen
I will return mute as the mermaid
who paid the price, cut out her tongue
for love of the upper world

        amends amends

    the brutal human tribe
for love. I am still
      thinking it over.

At rock bottom, holding a shell
to my waterlogged ear, I hear
the sigh of horses in a meadow
whistle of goldfinches breezing through thistle

far above   the white bottom of your boat,
frenzy of dragnet.
        O my anonymous,
my friend who believes
from here the twelve apologies
are like unto grains of sand,
forgive me: I have no higher power,
shadow of the valley, bottom of the sea.

Intervention

for Lara, for Cameron, for Anon, Anon, Anon

And now we learn that those interventions
we forced you to actually made things worse.
Brutal, to get you in to detox, brutal, the meetings
where your face was blank as a rock under clear water
and you promised never again. Brutal disruption,
brutal expense, as everything stopped
while we muscled you in there, forced
health and sobriety upon you. When you went
back to your best friend and your lover
when you abandoned us, we made wise choices
we kept clear boundaries, we disengaged
changed the locks. Now
evidence shows that an addict
is better kept close, treated with kindness.
This is said to be a revolutionary breakthrough.
We did not do well to yell in your face, to demand
abstinence with no substitution for your pain.
We harmed you with tough love,
shamed you. There was a reason you used
and we didn't want to hear it. Too late
to make amends: you died
and we refused your grave, your funeral
your letters, your lovely silver flasks, hidden
throughout the house. You were too greathearted
to get through life sober,
with nothing to blunt life's pain,
no hemlock, no purple-stained mouth,
no nightingale, no wine.
We stay, our hearts hard enough to keep
beating through the beating.

Stripped of the Legends

Stripped of the legends
stripped of vows &
stripped of addictions

it might be appropriate to ask
what can be kept?

O I forgot: stripped of faith
stripped of courage
stripped of ceremony from the old countries

it might be time to ask
how to go on?

Go in. Go into the city at first light
where you can see them:
lesbians in the mist, foraging for lattes
dervishing dogwalkers in orange safety vests
pulled in all directions by a dozen leashes.
Zombie father guiding a crying carriage
around the block ten times like a prayer.

Go farther in. Past the raccoon on the bin,
past a man picking up trash with tongs,
past the dump truck with its load of live tilapia
gasp-churning in the gutter, screaming gulls,
fishmongers in rubber aprons
sluicing fish into buckets
while that one lady with bees in her hair
rocks a Pekingese. If you catch their smiles
you can keep them.

Go all the way in. Buy yellow roses
from the woman with no shoes.
It is the time of contraction & dilation.

Stripped of membranes
stripped of language &
without a compass, without a ring,
surely we have come to the last stage
of labour, surely the new myth is being born.
The waters are breaking. It is the passion, com-

passion. So far in
there is no returning.

Ars Poetica

It is hard won, it is fragile, it does not bring joy.
It holds water, it holds air, it is its own reward.
It is light as cobweb, it is tough as cobweb, it is barely visible.
It is hollow as a victory in the battlefield.
It is heavy as a baby's coffin, great as a dolphin's eye.
It beckons, it whispers, it flickers in the wind.
It is impractical, it is laughable, it wrestles.
It is free, it is precious, it speaks the sound of water.
It is mad, it is alchemy, it is fleeting and enduring.
It can be studied but it can't be learned by heart.
It can be followed in the forest but only by its track.
It can be followed in the city but only by its blood.
It jumps fences, it embroiders, it ferries the dead.
It can't be captured and it has no price.
It's in the screaming alley, the ink-blot pines, the village well.
On the threshold of your pain you may find it
holding the door ajar like a rock
and if you do you will lift it, weigh it, curse it
and say it is not enough.
It is enough.

Feast

The table is set with stars. Come to the table.
Put away your anger and your guitar.
The apples are baking. Tallow drips from candles.

Nothing can hold back death. Come to the table.
Set your burnt spoon aside in a difficult drawer.
Wipe the wine from your mouth. Come as soon as you're able.

The wheat's in the barn and the barge. The babe's in the cradle.
The history that led to the railway cars
is a trunk you can leave at the dock. Unbridle, unsaddle

the dappled horse in your barefooted fable
the horse that you rode to the battle, and then to the wars.
The salmon's been pulled from the sea, and served with its shadow.

Come to the table, beloved, the three-legged table,
for you are the bell jar's hammer, the broken-down door.
What's crooked finds balance on matchbooks and elbows.

O prodigal child. O sage of the bluegrass piano!
The buckets catch buckshot that falls from a bonfire of stars.
You were stabbed in both hands by the bees that you robbed in the grotto.
We'll serve halos of moon-mist, we'll capture tornados in jars. Come to the table.

Acknowledgements

I am grateful to the following people for their support in writing this manuscript: Alayna Munce, George Elliott Clarke, Ellen Bass, Ann Dowsett Johnston, Leslie Walker Williams, Susan Elmslie, Marge Piercy, Elee Kraljii Gardiner, Masarah Van Eyck and Isabelle Fieschi.

From "Flood": "Do I still yearn for my virginity?" from *If Not, Winter, Fragments of Sappho*, translated by Anne Carson. This poem was commissioned by Oolichan Books for the forthcoming anthology, *Tag: Canadian Poets at Play*. The line, "before what we now know came," is from the poem, "Above the Alberta Floods," by John Barton, who tagged me.

"Sunflowers" makes reference to Robert Frost's poem, "Nothing Gold Can Stay."

"Living on Islands": title in homage to the book, *Living on Islands*, by Robert Rose.

The epigraph from "Tooth" is from Lynn Strongin's *The Burn Poems* (Headmistress Press, 2015).

"Honey" was inspired by the artist Blake Little's photographs.

Also appeared in:
> "Flood": *Plentitudes* and *Tag: An Anthology of Canadian Poets at Play*
> "Confusion," "Cleave": *CV2*
> "A Wedding Ghazal": *The Lavender Review*
> "Golden Age": *Eighteen Bridges*
> "Living on Islands I" (formerly titled "White Lilies"): *Prism International*
> "Nitpicking": *Alaska Quarterly Review*
> "Bees": *Tar River Poetry*
> "Corona for Charlotte," "Good Measure," "Sunflowers": *The Fiddlehead*

Rachel Rose is a dual American/Canadian citizen whose work has appeared in various journals in Canada, the US, New Zealand and Japan, including *Poetry*, *The Malahat Review* and *The Best American Poetry*, as well as several anthologies. Her most recent poetry collection, *Song & Spectacle* (2012), won the Audre Lorde Award in the US and the Pat Lowther Award in Canada. She was the librettist for *When the Sun Comes Out*, an opera that grapples with fundamentalism and forbidden love. It premiered in Vancouver in 2013 and in Toronto in 2014. She is the winner of the Peterson Memorial Prize for poetry and the Bronwen Wallace award for fiction, and has won the Pushcart Prize twice. She is the Poet Laureate of Vancouver for 2014–2017.